SUGAR

Steve Szewczok

NeoPoiesis Press, LLC

NeoPoiesis Press

Inquiries:
P.O. Box 38037
Houston, TX 77238-8037

Primary Address:
2775 Harbor Ave SW, Suite D
Seattle, WA 98126-2138

www.neopoiesispress.com

Steve Szewczok – Sugar
ISBN 978-0-9855577-1-3 (paperback : alk. paper)
        1. Poetry. I. Szewczok, Steve

Printed in the United States of America.

First Edition

for those who struggle

Contents

The Catalyst

I remember the taste of floor wax
Tiny splinters in my small hands
Kept me from praying that night
I knew then God was useless to me
I knew then He was gone

I remember the sound of my father's voice
He was a musician a singer a composer
He sang to me of a loss
I could not understand
His rough music
His intonations
I was a child

I was alone at nine
My sister and me
She was four
I loved her so much

Our mother moved us far away
A new start
A new life

I felt like a fugitive

As if I had done
Something wrong
Something criminal

It was my fault wasn't it?

I was the catalyst

Wonder years

I remember the cold feel of brick
The solitude of vacant corridors
The smell of boys
The curiosity of girls
The sound of nicotine caressing lungs
The secret hideaways of double dares
The first male hand touching my breasts
I was so frightened so very afraid
I didn't want to disappoint him
I wanted him to like me
I knew first hand
How a man's hate
Can destroy a woman's trust
I have eyes
I see things

I know bad things happen to good people
I wasn't born yesterday
I'm not stupid

I remember the taste of floor wax
I can't forget it

Sometimes when I hide away

No one can find me

Not even me

My life was perfect

I was perfect

But that never brought him back

So fuck it!!

It was a 1973-Ford Capri
Brown with tan interior
Real vinyl seats   *smooth*
Four speed manuel tranny

Overhead cam Holly Webber carb
She could tap out at 135 MPH
He had Heart's *Dreamboat Annie* playing
When his finger first entered me
I came

So did he

We were built by the same mismanagements

Neither one of us trusted anyone

He'd been fucked so many times by his uncle
he thought he might be gay

I put an end to that
You might say I saved him
But then
So did he... *save me*

I was 14
He was 17
But he did think
I was 16

I lied

I told you I **was** perfect
But **now** - *Fuck it!!*

It was late spring
There was a lake
We used to go up there a lot
It was quiet
No sound
But for our own sweat on vinyl
Our own tremblings through the foggy interiors
Of our sexuality

He was my introduction to

My first cigarette

My first beer (tastes like floor wax YUCK)
My first shot of vodka (YUM)
My first joint
Everything

In late spring at the lake
He gave me a new life:

My first hit of crystal meth!

The Traveler

I remember the feel of the wet road in my hands

The smell of self-destruction
In this city

But

That was not me

I'm not ready to destruct

This was *My* new start
        My new life
        My new city

        I can handle anything

Daddy's Girl

I remember his hands holding me
My body loaded like a gun
I wanted to go off on him
To let him know my rage
To give back 10 years
Of him
Gone

But I had come to him
I found him not broken
He told me
He loved me

Loved me?

What am *I* to do with *that?*

It's too late in this world for dialogue

Grandma's House

I wear the sign of Gemini around my neck

To remind me
I am not alone

There are two of us

One
    I hold in capture
Two
    I ache for in the bleeding rain

But
    At least I have a roof over my head

Daddy lets me *live* here

It was Grandma's house

She's been dead now 10 years

10 years?

A lifetime for the sum of us.

It's my home now

The smells all belong to me

The dried vomit
The blood stained rags
The burnt toast
The soured milk on the floor
Strawberry jam between my toes
Sticky
It's sticky in here

My carpet is aluminum foil

My shelves are gallon vodka bottles in perfect balance

The art on my wall is my novel

I've been writing it for 5 years now

It's my memoirs of God

How I slept with the humanity of Him

I stand on my bed
I trampoline bounce

I reach
beyond
the ceiling
          past
                    the bleeding rain

This I will carry past my drunken star-shining

I was to be beautiful
I was to become a movie star
I was to have *it* all

When my book is published
I will get it all back

I will

Three Days Earlier

Prologue:

1 positive + 1 positive + 2 positives
Equals 4 good things minus
1 negative – 1 negative – 2 negatives
= nothing
Fuck
1 positive minus 1 negative
How can that be? How can that fit?
How can you take a positive from a negative?

I slink my way to the corner
I look up to see a sign
I look down and find change

On the ground

It's never enough

I hang out in front of what I want
I ask strange men to buy me
Alcohol
Vodka
Lots of vodka
Keeps me   balanced
We all need   *balance* in our lives

The odd time I suck a cock
When they cum in my mouth
They all taste like floor wax

Whatever
I get what I want

It gets me to work on time

(Pre)ᵃᵐᵇˡᵉ ~~then work~~)

Gluten arband mina frau

Do you smoke my stogies in bed
?
I like to keep my poison close
I would not want to stray   *far*

Who's going to save my soul   *now*
?

The absence of evidence
is not the same as
the evidence of absence
even I know that

These ain't magic beans I sow in my garment
It takes work to sustain life

Yeah VERK I must VERK Yeah
?

VerK it makes me feel zoh horny

Dancing

I love dancing on the faces of strange men

Pressing their lonely lives into my chest

Wrapping my sticky pussy around their chipped shoulders

I bring safe haven

I carry you until you cum in your Armani slacks

I remember dancing on grandma's floor

The chassé gliding easily by the taste of floor wax

Dreaming

I remember the endless banging of the sea
I hoped that you would not hurt me
Hearing the rage of the ocean
I feel your spume frothing about my mouth

I sit beached next to 79 whales
All dying from exhaustion
I sit and hear the last of the whale songs
How I wish my father were with me
He would understand their music

I dig my dulled nails into the skin of the beach

Trying to sharpen my claws

Trying to count the grains before the hourglass is up

I dig until I bleed

The smell of my blood mixes with the dying whales' song

A pas de deux of chaos

A taste I can't get away from

I wake up every morning to memory

Silver Jubilee

The beast I know
Is trying to breathe
Through its back
Thin razor cuts
Form the gills

As I celebrate my lover
this gorgeous afternoon
I go to our lake

So quiet here. So quiet.
Nothing runs away from here. Nothing
I look along the shoreline I see...

What?

That cannot be
Brown rusted metal
It's our Capri?=!

She sits like a queen out here
The lake her only subject
I worm my way closer
The windows still stained from our cum and nicotine

Our initials carved into its body as a heart
I pry open a door
I time machine back twenty five years

I return

To sweat on vinyl seats
To his finger in my pussy
To the taste of floor wax
To my first hit of crystal meth.

He called me Sugar!

Hypnosis

The closest I can get to the earth
is the floor
I scrunch my face into sidewalk cracks
I do lines under the aluminum carpet

Trying to finish my book: "Goddess"

She is a hypnotist

I am her savior

Collecting bottles

When I dip myself in chocolate
I bury me under nine inch nails
I caravan through dead streets
Collecting the month's rent
Collecting the water's bill
Collecting the light's heat

I don't want to freeze

When I flip myself off
I've had enough of you
You need to get me high
You need to get me drunk
You need to get me savage

That's the way of our wild

Get your fucking dogs out of my pussy
Bring me some meat

Take these emptied bottles with you

Nothing comes of nothing

A perfect dozen

My sister comes by
She tries the rehab line
I say no, no, no!

Not that ole song and dance

She brings donuts in a box
I just want the box

My sister speaks to me like I'm a fucking retard

Does anyone really know what that fucking means?

I'm not a fucking retard

I'm a clairvoyant

I see the sewage from shit souls

"There must be a dozen donuts here."
 I said

She said,
"Actually, thirteen"

"Thirteen? That isn't twelve.
Twelve is a dozen."

"Yes, but thirteen is a perfect dozen.
It's a baker's dozen, perfect"

"Yeah well, just leave me the box."

It makes me feel like a gift

Heavenly day

I need beauty in skin
Like the olive needs the gin

I walked away in silence
A long time ago

When my head hit the floor
I was nine

My memories were of floor wax
and Father

Today,
My confusions are much older
I remember the way day broke back then
Like a wild stallion caged in regret
It's not something you ever forget—

The abandonment of

School plays
Dance recitals in June
Birthdays
Spelling bees
Christmas

Time is a liar

A cheat

A proverbial wolf

It heals nothing
Ever
Never
Ever
Heals Nothing

We're all Pieces of April forever lost in May

Candlelight

I remember scraping my knees

The flesh calls for atonement of my skin

[adunamentum]

Give me unity

Let me hide behind the wick
Underneath the wax
Beyond this ole flame

My book is almost finished

I just need to clear the wax off the walls

And seal

My heart

With poison kisses
And
Coffin nails
And
Pillows from china
And
Spices from India
And
Beautiful Russian brides by order

i could eat me one right now

Caged

I remember the draining of red pomegranates

The seeds sparkle when you plug them in
Lite-brite
Blinds the sight in your dreams

I'm here with Evil
Contemplating
Squeezing oranges out of their juice
Mixing it with the vodka veins
Screwdrivers and sunglasses

All the pain of young baby's breath

A world of fools

By this point
I am my own church

My own religion patronizes me
I'm the patron of lost womanhood
I am my savior when I fall
I belong to my habits
That's how deep my love is

My soul?

That boat sails

In a world of fools

Laundry day

It's like a disease
The way I keep messin' up
Keep spilling things on my clothes
You think I would learn by now
I want to be the best I can
But I adore the cliché I have become
I've survived millennia

You could travel the country on the tracks of my arms

Who knows your birthday?
Who knows your highest?
Who knows numbers?

Who loves you from the bottom?

These cotton fabrics do

These denim maps I wear around my legs

These silk panties lead my pussy back to my sexuality

And

No matter how many times I do the wash

I can't get me out of this T-shirt

The one Momma bought me

The one with my name on it

New world

I remember me as a speck of dust
Flirting my way around your globe
I remember the taste of your sweat
The smell of here and now
The hell of then and there

I was powder up your nose
I was liquid love in your veins

I was goddess

I ruled your cock with a wicked mouth

I ran with no one
I behaved badly
I'm sorry

I should have let you blow out the candles
But
I didn't want anyone's wishes affecting me

I like this world too much
I don't want to change skin

Not this late in the day

Cancer

I twist as smoke around the belly of the serpent
I practice my part by living
I'm directed by feel good
I don't swim in madness any more
I don't know how they can call this a *dis-ease*

I don't feel any *dis-ease*

I couldn't care less if there are clouds in hell

In my world

Death is in remission

The facts of life

I don't leech anymore
That's for the blood letters
L. O. V. and E.

My Romance:
Cigarettes and coffee

My teeth:
Yellow from too much sun

I've been sittin' here
Drinkin' aftershave

My breath smells great

Under my tongue
I hideaway fugitives

You'd be surprised
What you can hide under there

It's how they bring the bombs in

I should put some flowers in my hair
They're pretty

It's been so long since I've seen pretty

This is no place for a paper doll

I'll find a way Mamma

I'll find a way to see you again

I promise

I remember the taste of the floor wax Mamma!

I remember

Breaking the rules

Meet me by the water
Don't forget your net
We might go fishing
And a bucket
Take a bucket
For the clams
And a plunger
In case the ocean gets stuck

We'll need a way out of these sewers

Fuck honey you're growin'
Getting big
Alligator big
Your skin's been travelin'

I've been waiting for you by the water

The whales have all gone

I don't expect anything

Just meet me meet me meet me

Come back to my arms one last time

I'm tired of looking for you in newspapers and magazines

Cake

I flip
A
Coin
I have no control
With what you steal
Tell the world about me
And fuck off
You'll get no tax receipts from me
I ain't no charity ball
No benefit concerting in this house
What?!
I see
You brought a cake
You remembered
Fuck!
You remembered
Great
Now *I* have to remember
Five zero
Five zero
5   0
50
Fuck I'm fifty

How the fuck did I make it to fifty?

Stoic Poses

I become a lens in this world

You send me light

I bend towards your shape

I am photograph

I am a point of view

My choices are my carrying place

It is where my Carrion flesh shrivels

After the gold rush I become heroine

I seep around sounds and syllables

I imprint my skin on the walls of my novel

I lean against the backside of the church

Where the stones come alive

Where those stoic faces move on dead lips

They all smell the same way

They all say the same thing

The dead will out live us all

Blueberries

I remember my sister on mother's back
Maybe she was 9 months

I remember the feel of the rich soil
I remember thinking how fun it must be

To become dirt
Lay around all day drinking in the rain

Watching everyone grow up around you
It seemed perfect

It seemed right

I remember crawling down-low
The first time I shot heroin

I dreamed of blueberry patches
I remembered Mamma and sister picking blueberries
I remembered me
Wanting to become Dirt

Careful what you wish for

Influenza (break-down immunity)

My body is shrinking by degrees
I would try and move mountains
But today I'm living underwater
Inside my living room
The sun bakes under my skin
I swim in the icy ocean of bathtub
I collapse in accordion breath
I just want to be high
I just want to get drunk

I just want to evolve into Sugar

Cat Fish

I sink
My eyes upon fish tank

It was a gift

I put a catfish in it

I've always wanted a cat but I can't stand the hair
So I bought me a catfish

I call it CAT
It sinks never floats

It sits on the bottom-eyeing houseflies
I can see its lips quivering

I can feel the stitches starting to tug

Last week
I was cleaning out the litter
And
The fucking thing scratched me

Five stitches across my eye.

See?

Fucking cat fish

Boundaries

Beyond the sunny border

I look into a gallon jug of vodka

My throat soothes as the liquid covers my hard palette

Fills my mouth with prescribed sunshine

I can hear the ocean in my ears

I can circumnavigate around my frozen puddle veins

Through the great locks and channels of my being

As I crawl into an immaculate opening of space

Shampoo

I run my fingers by touch
They lift through the veil of my hair
I have the hands of a mechanic
Grease stained and salvaged
Broken up

I put me back together

These are the building blocks

The essentials of my completeness

In Bloom

I soak my feet
In the waters
Of the underworld

I see things
Beyond
The shadowy edges of dusk

I've risen out of the dead many times
It ignites me to phoenix-like
It separates me like an Idea

A scaffold of structuring in bloom

The Edge

How happy I am
Here
Living in the dark

I say what is true and clean

I make my devotions to the secret and underground

I am a hushed weight about to fall

I am drunken starlight at the end of sight

No reason to look up

I will never wave to you

I walk in good company

In Eclipse

Turn to the lost souls
Ride the mist till morning lifts
Skate the ice veins to my heart

Pretend I can't be seen
Kiss me in the rain
I want to be a movie star

Keep your eye on the dance lover
Don't worry
Once in a death-time

I'll remember you in my dream

Marathon

Mile after mile after mile after mile after mile
The 1970's flash by BYE
I don't play games
I don't rush on anywhere
I keep no pictures
Only a tin of Johnson's Floor wax
It's all the memory I need
I know where I am
It was an accident Mamma
It was my elbow that betrayed me

I remember the milk laughing
All the way down to floor

I remember Rosie crying

Why Mamma?

I was nine
I was nine

I adored you how!

There were stars in my night back then

I whistled for Daddy to come
I remember the open hand
Catching up with my right cheek
I whistled for Daddy to come

I could taste the floor wax
Off her angry hand

Why Mamma?

I was nine
I was nine

I adored you how!

Watch and see how I run!

Kicking dogs

I'm a corpse who does not know death

Living down below is really nowhere

If we believe in the fight
We're already saved

So go ahead
Kick a dog

Chase down tumbleweeds

Chapter 13, Sybil

I've a gypsy heart

I speak through the gods

I perform madness

That's my trick

You don't want to know the future

How we all starve through the next drought

This Gasoline thing is only the beginning

JUST WAIT! You don't know worse like I know worse

Believe in me when I say It's going there...

We will fight to eat

We will kill to drink

We will not become savages

We already are   *wild boars*

I was born out of legend

What I see is yours

What Eye see
What eye sees?

This city?

It still smells of destruction

Extinction

I live in the gutter just below the curb
My friends are the ants
They carry me along this river of filth
They clean my house
They eat away the waste of me
I think they love me
But then
Love is purely a subjective emotion
I love getting high
It is all that I live for

Nothing else

Nothing matters

Dinosaurs
I miss them
I loved them
They understand
Extinction

As do I

Dinosaurs?

You could say they protect me.

Crash and Reboot

I drink shampoo out of the bottle
It cleanses me
I feel clean. I feel right.

I squeeze a lemon to death

I strangle it with my fingers thick with thinking

I give the lemon Aid

I resuscitate the citrus through my drinking
I revive having a conscience
I choose to reboot

I choose to back up my hard disc one vertebra at a time

I roll to standing

Before the market crash
Before they burned down Rome
Before the ice age melted in the glass of my world

Arrivals

A pinprick two pronged
A space odyssey
A time machine
A crack pipe
My old library card
A Band-Aid
A ruptured liver
A punctured lung
A wishing well
My old library card

At the station the train-master helps the dead to arrivals

At the Station

A living truth
A microscopic microbe
A trackside bet
A human (liquidation) clearance sale
Balloon transportation for hire
A poppy on Veteran's Day
Or an opium den giveaway

Remembering things past
Like:

Milk
And floor wax

Vodka
And crystal meth

Sport cars
And Death

At the station the train-master reads
the palms of the departed

Good things

Good things happen to good people

Well I'm good people and it didn't happen to me

I'd slit your fuckin' throat for a dollar
I'll suck the cum out of your cock tail
Just to quench my thirst

Good things happen to good people

Well I'm good people but it didn't happen to me

You can fuck me in my crack whore ass
If you promise to beat me up OH, I like it HARD

Good things happen to good people

Well I'm good people and it didn't happen to me

I'm good people and it didn't happen to me

good people and it didn't happen to me

people and it didn't happen to me

and it didn't happen to me

it didn't happen to me

didn't happen to me

happen to me

to me

me

Pieces

If you kill the body the head is dead
Scattered bits of glass shatter eyes
The windows to this soul lay in the pains
Busted through todays and tomorrows
I can't get enough of what I need
It *will* kill me
I know that
But
I don't care enough

To pick up the pieces

Shattered

Seagulls come in from the storm

They swarm around the garbage of what I have become

My body swims the ocean in fear of drowning

I am not fish
I am not human

I am not what I wanted
Not anymore

My tits unravel
My pussy can't fetch a dime

My mouth lives in dirt
Under a soiled tongue

I am stunted outwitted

Someone has stolen my invincibility

I am leftover drug abuse
I am a child of hate

I was born by mistake
By accident I was told

Now at least you know

How it feels to be shattered

The Ring

In a fairy tale
Long ago
I came out firing leather

I was a champion
I was top form
I was first prize

Blue ribbon
Undefeated
Undefined

Raw potential
A natural talent
Yes

In a fairy tale
Long ago
I had everything a girl could want

Cocaine
Heroin
Crystal meth

Vodka
Lots of vodka
And

I lived happily ever fucking after

Disappearance

I carry my bones lightly
I carry my heart here next to a picture of my father
I carry my lungs past breathing
I fill them with shit
I empty them closer to death
I carry the fire in my hands
I search for more cave dwellings
I like the ones with the crazy pictures on the walls
I spend my time fucking up
I sing in colors
Red and blue
Green and yellow
Pink and purple
That's the way I see music
Like a contusion on the soul

How small can love get?

Defective

Shadows flood my room
I break all mirrors
I don't want to be seen
The iceberg sits in stillness
Waiting for the snowfall

But this is Los Angeles
We have plenty of greasy sunlight
But no snow falls here
Not in the fields of make believe

The march of my flesh is conquered
By the weight of my frailty
All you Romans with big cocks
Come fuck me
I am Cleopatra on the lamb
I am Caesar on my salad

I am the shadow
That floods my sky
I am the pasted wax
On floors
I am wasteland

I am wasteland

Jail/Homecoming

Being in jail is like starring in your own porn flick

It's my favorite place to be (with the exception of Grandma's house

I love it in here
I get fed three circular meals a day
My nose is never clean
I get to wax as many floors as I want
I'm high all the time
I get to eat as much pussy as I want

One of the girls fucks me with her *ginormous* cock

This is my heaven

So Mister Judge!

You think you can intimidate ultimatums to me!

"Finish another rehab program or go to jail for two years.."

Fuck You! Bring it on!

I could use a nice vacation.

Rehab

I am mired down to drowning in this muck

There are many in here who go out early in their bones

Trying to escape into the new dawn of tomorrow

I have been clean and sober now for thirty-one days

I have seen the light

I am all woman
I am a superhero
I am saved saved saved
Rescued from my loss
I have been found as human

Time to make escape

I'll hitch a ride on the next cloud that rolls by

There's got to be a cloudy day in here somewhere

I'll find it

And once I do

There will be
Floor wax under my skin

There will be
Acid in my rain

There will be
Lines of snow cut across my mirrored valley

There will be
Russians in my bottle

There will be
Hell to pay forward

Gone Bye Bye

The ocean I live in died today

Gone bye bye

The sense that I had of ever being loved

Gone bye bye

Now, I'm found on my knees
Trying to give this world a *blow-job*
Trying to revive what I know of kindness

I can't wash him out of my skin

Gone bye bye

The air I breathe today
Is lost
Is grief
Is misplaced rage

This is the day all music of the world weeps

For Daddy
Gone

Bye bye

Affliction

I wish to be a pillow

Something that might suffocate my shadow in sleep

I am dominos tumbling

I have slow-cooked me

Stewed meat of many years over

I could eat the heart of my matter

You can serve me up as a plague of trouble

I don't mind

Here are the ruins of my persona

The pillars of my sexuality collapse into sand

And

I am in mountains

I am in-grained

I am never coming down

Floor Wax

I run to the bottom of my life
I scratch and claw kick and hit

I am on my knees here!!
Trying to lift forty-nine years
Of dirt from this floorboard

I was nine when I first hit this spot
Run your finger along here
You can feel the tooth mark I left behind

We were all here at Grandma's house

My mother was waxing this floor

I remember the smell
Of apple pie baking in Grandma's oven
I remember the glossy blue tiled floor
Screaming clean!

I used to pretend
It was the ocean

My baby blue blanket
I would spread on the floor

She was a good boat
She never let me sink or fall over
She was always dependable

I remember Bobby Darin
Singing *Mack The Knife*
On the radio

I can still hear those footsteps
Coming up the lane
The creak of my father's Wallaby shoes
The rumble of thunder nearing

Storms a brewin'
Lightning is about to strike down hard

Daddy's home!

I remember the scent of someone unfamiliar
A perfume perhaps I don't know

Daddy was wearing someone else's skin
There was a peculiar silence in the air

Mamma stayed down close to the floor
She would stare a hole right through Daddy

I remember Daddy saying,

I'll be leaving...

I screamed the lights out!
I ran towards daddy

I sailed across oceans trying to reach him
I remember nothing but mama's floor waxed hand across
my face

I remember Daddy picking me up off the floor
My lip bleeding my father's loss

I wanted to stop him
What could I have done?

I said
May I have the next dance Daddy?
            No
No?

You broke me that night Daddy

When I fell I broke
How could I mend
You didn't want me

YOU DID NOT WANT ME!

I'm sorry Mamma

53

I'm sorry
I wasn't a better daughter

I just didn't give a fuck about anything

Except being fifty story's high
You know it wasn't the high
That I was addicted to

It was the danger I was addicted to

I'm sorry Rosie
I wish I could have been your big sister
But I'm just no good

There's a strange odor about
Someone's skin perhaps
I don't know

There is a carousel softly turning
There is someone driving a large nail
Into the side of my head

Jesus!

I remember my head hitting down
My right front tooth
Found its mark on the floor

I wish I were high right now
I think I shit my pants!
I can taste the floor wax

I can hear it
California rain
Is falling

I am fifty-eight today
Happy birthday

Sugar baby

Psalm of Rosie

This is the first time
I've seen you sober
It only took your death
What else could it have taken?

There's something very primal
About this.
You fucker!

You fucking cunt!

You left me with no one!

I'm alone

Fuck! ALONE!

You break me Sugar.
I'm broken in to bits of you.
Now what do I do?

Sugar, What do I do?

About the Author

Steve Szewczok stems from the island of Cape Breton, Nova Scotia on the east coast of Canada. With a background in theatre and music, Steve has performed in over 50 theatrical productions as well as working in radio and film and writing for the theatre. Steve currently lives in Montreal with his two children and works on the production side of the film industry. *Sugar* is Steve's debut book of poetry. He is currently working on his second collection of poems.

Acknowledgements

I would very much like to thank the following for their support in the creating of this work:

Dale Winslow

William T Marshe

Glynis Ranny

Brian McKay
Wesley Long
Ed MacDonald
Rosamond Pyke

Thomas Latizeau-Szewczok (for all your wondrous imagination, thank you Son.)

All the MySpace poets who moved me to write again;
Blackbird, Will, Francoise, Gillian, Analept, Seb
and Tami St Germain for her support.

Finally a big thank you goes to;

NeoPoiesis Press
And
Helena Bonham Carter (Thanks for reading the first copy and thank you for your kind words.)

NeoPoiesis: *a new way of making*

1) in ancient Greece, poiesis referred to the process of making: creation - production - organization - formation - causation

2) a process that can be physical and spiritual, biological and intellectual, artistic and technological, material and teleological, efficient and formal

3) a means of modifying the environment and a method of organizing the self, the making of art and music and poetry, the fashioning of memory and history and philosophy, the construction of perception and expression and reality

4) an independent publisher with a steadfast goal to print and promote outstanding poets, writers and artists that reflect the creative drive and spirit of the new electronic landscape

NeoPoiesisPress.com